John Jacobs Analyses Golf's Superstars

John Jacobs Analyses Golf's Superstars

Written in collaboration with Ken Bowden

Stanley Paul – London

Stanley Paul & Company Ltd.
3 Fitzroy Square, London W1

London Melbourne Sydney Auckland
Wellington Johannesburg Cape Town
and agencies throughout the world

First published 1974
© John Jacobs and Ken Bowden

Set in 'Monophoto' Ehrhardt

Printed photolitho in Great Britain by
Ebenezer Baylis & Son Ltd.
The Trinity Press, Worcester, and London

ISBN 0 09 118270 0

Contents

John Jac

Introduction

It is my sincere wish that you will get tremendous enjoyment and technical help from the photographic sequences we have put together in this book, depicting the swing actions of many of the world's finest golfers.

If you choose to use these pictures, and my analyses of them, to try to improve your own game, I would ask you to remember four things.

First, note that if these great golfers have one thing in common it is that they all *hit the ball in time*. They do not hit 'late,' or 'early,' but all deliver the clubhead to the ball on a wide enough approach path to enable it to move the ball directly *forward* by hitting it solidly in the *back*. By comparison, many a run-of-the-mill golfer, having got into a late-hit position, fails to *release*, thereby obliging himself to deliver the club to the ball on a weak, narrow, chopping approach path.

Secondly, take into account that these golfers, like all truly successful sportsmen, are more than great technicians; they are also great *competitors*. The more I've seen of golf, the more I have become convinced that technique is not more than 50 per cent of the game. Given a reasonably reliable long game, and an effective short game, how successful a golfer any individual becomes depends much more on his or her desire, tenacity, intelligence and self-control than on matters of swing style or form. This point is much overlooked, or ignored, by the club player.

Third, never lose sight of the fact, in studying these or other pictures, that the still camera cannot capture the *action* of the golf swing. The positions in which the camera has 'stopped' the players here are not artificially attained. They are simply positions that the players *move through* during the intensely lively motion of the overall swing.

Fourth, and finally, please remember that, although it is possible to gain much useful knowledge about golf technique from the printed word and image, in the last analysis there is no substitute for personal instruction from a competent teacher.

Play well and have fun.

John Jacobs

Jack Nicklaus

Tremendously strong and immensely gifted

Profile

If there is one man in golf today to whom the overworked word super-star truly applies, it has to be Jack Nicklaus. His already phenomenal golf game just seems to keep getting better and better – and, considering what Jack has achieved thus far, that's almost awe-inspiring to contemplate.

In 1972, Nicklaus's best year to date, he won an incredible seven tournaments out of nineteen played, and placed second in three more. His US tour earnings for the year, $320 542, set an all-time record, and were over $100 000 ahead of his closest pursuer. Disappointed as he was not to have won the Grand Slam, Jack could take some solace from the fact that in this year he became undisputably the world's number one golfer – some were saying the greatest golfer of all time.

Nicklaus's career has been rich in reward, beginning with his US Amateur victories in 1959 and 1961. Since joining the tour in 1962, he has won three US Opens, four Masters, three PGA Championships and two British Opens. His total of fourteen major championships has been approached only by the immortal Bobby Jones with 13. Nicklaus had racked up a total of 50 US tour victories by November, 1973, at which point he was thirty-three years old.

With total career earnings of $1 718 997 at the end of 1972 – easily the highest in golfing history – Nicklaus isn't yet ready to turn his total attention to his family, tennis, fishing, his extensive world-wide business interests, or even his great love of golf course architecture. The Grand Slam, and any other records the game may offer, will keep him enthusiastic for as long as he feels he can maintain his game at peak physical condition.

One of the world's longest-ever straight hitters, Nicklaus was obviously destined for stardom while still in his early teens – he first broke seventy at thirteen years of age. But over the years there have been many refinements in and improvements to his game, with which in some areas – like wedge play and chipping – he is still dissatisfied. In recent years he has also watched his galleries grow fantastically, to the point where the longer-haired, thinner and altogether more handsome Jack Nicklaus, deeply appreciative of his new appeal, has won over even the fans who had pulled against him during the early part of his career in favour of the then more charismatic Arnold Palmer.

Although essentially a modest and at times even a retiring man, Nicklaus privately believes that he can improve his game for at least another five years, given only sufficient desire to compete. At present he has that in spades, if for no other reason than that it embarrasses him to play poorly, especially in major tournaments.

Such improvements will be made largely in the physical areas of golf. For a number of years now Jack has been a masterly strategist and tactician, with an ultra-intelligent and ultra-realistic approach to course management. He has massive confidence in himself, and an almost formidable ability to wrap himself in a cocoon of concentration on the course. The placing of his business affairs under his own control, with the help of a partner and a team of specialists, has added vastly to his peace of mind.

It is thus difficult indeed to envisage this particular king vacating his castle for at least another decade.

Ken Bowden

1

2

3

Analysis

The qualities of champions are easily recognizable, but always difficult to define. Jack Nicklaus epitomises those qualities, as did Bobby Jones, and I believe they have had many things in common, not least their tremendous natural gifts for golf, their intelligence, their intense competitive spirit, their powerful sense of sportsmanship and fair play, and their commonsense approach to shot-making.

If Jack has a quirk, it is his occasional show of intolerance, perhaps born of his comparative lack of experience of failure. But that is easily forgiven, particularly by one like me, who is now old enough to recognize that he has long had the same fault.

Turning now to Jack's technique, I think the most formative thing that ever happened to him was the joint decision he made with his life-long teacher and mentor, Jack Grout, that if one day Nicklaus was to become a great player he must be able to hit the ball a very long way. The result of this admirable decision was the development of a very big, full, hard-hitting action: a massive turn of the body going back and through, allied to a thrusting, sky-reaching swing of the arms.

Grout wanted length and height first, believing that control and

4　　　　　　　　　　　　　　5　　　　　　　　　　　　　6

accuracy could come later, and I couldn't agree more with his philosophy, especially in so far as youngsters are concerned (Nicklaus started golf under Grout at age ten). Throughout my own teaching career I have seen so many 14-to-18-year-olds, playing to low handicaps, whose actions were so restricted as to leave no room for later improvement.

One of Nicklaus's greatest talents as he matured was his ability to win when not playing at his best – and in this respect his sheer power off the tee even, when slightly mishitting the ball, combined with his remarkably fine 'touch', have often saved his bacon.

At times I've seen Jack with his hands in the wrong (for him) position at the top of the backswing, which has created either a disrupting reaction in the downswing, or an awkwardness in delivering the clubface square to the swing line at impact, or both. But his biggest problems occur when his already extremely tilted shoulder turn becomes so tilted that the reciprocal tilt of the shoulders on the downswing forces him either to block his left side going through; or, if he clears the left side, to swing his shoulders out and over the ball, producing an outside-in clubhead path.

The former action, by restricting body clearance, forces the wrists to snap and roll too early, causing both hooked and pushed shots. It also militates against the correct ball-turf sequence with irons, and

7   8   9

may explain why Jack is occasionally a comparatively poor short-iron player.

The latter action – swinging the shoulders over the ball – forces a blocking of the hand action to prevent the ball being hit straight left. Nicklaus's superb hand-eye coordination and great physical strength occasionally enable him to get away with this action, even to the point of winning. But it is when he adds just a little more turn to his tilted shoulder action, and thus swings the club sufficiently inside the target line to promote full body clearance and clubhead release on the downswing, that he becomes unbeatable.

I believe a factor contributing to Jack's tendency to over-tilt his shoulders (he and I have discussed this aspect of his swing) is his low head position at address (frame 1). If you are a tilter instead of a turner, this is one aspect of Nicklaus's game you shouldn't copy – getting your chin up higher will set your shoulders in a much better turning position.

What many golfers could profitably copy from Jack, however, is the tilt of the chin to the right at the start of the backswing (frame 1), making room for a full shoulder turn and a free arm-swing; and also the straight-line left arm-club relationship, making for a one-piece takeaway.

Featuring as it does a huge shoulder turn (frames 3–6), allied to an

10   11   12

extremely wide and high arm swing (frames 3 and 5), and a very delayed cocking of the wrists (frame 4 related to frame 6), Nicklaus's backswing is beyond the physical capabilities of most weekend golfers. However, if you decide to give this kind of action a try, note especially Jack's full hip turn allied to his flexed right knee (frame 6).

In common with many great golfers, Nicklaus has extremely powerful legs, and frames 7 and 8 beautifully illustrate how effectively he uses them to initiate the downswing, with the sliding and turning action common to most top modern tournament professionals. But don't make the mistake of thinking that because Jack initiates the downswing with his legs he is not simultaneously swinging hard at the ball with his arms, hands and the clubhead – see frames 7–10. Note especially in frame 9 how the club is in position to be applied solidly to *the back* of the ball at ground level (frame 10).

Frame 11 is a superb illustration of the right shoulder passing under and through as the hips clear to make way for the arms to swing the club well through the ball, thereby eliminating exaggerated wrist-roll in the hitting area. In frame 12 the body, pulled by the momentum of the club, continues to unwind into a high, wide and handsome finish.

John Jacobs

13

Gene Littler

The perfect model for the club golfer

Profile

Gene Littler is a quiet, mild-mannered, wonderfully modest fellow, with a playing style as unobtrusive as his personality. But both his game and character possess a lot more steel than might be immediately noticeable. Littler has been playing the US pro tour now for two decades, and his achievements have been impressive. He has almost always been a contender in any tournament he enters, and he has gained the respect and – even harder to achieve – the friendship of his fellow pros.

When he joined the pro tour in 1954, Littler held the 1953 US Amateur crown. As a professional, he has had 20 US tour victories, including the 1961 US Open and the 1965 Canadian Open, and has rarely placed out of the money, as is evident in his career earnings – at the end of 1972 he had collected $825 967 in prize money and stood seventh in the all-time money winners' list at that time.

Gene wasn't on the tour much during 1972. In March of that year he was operated on for cancer. A malignant tumour and lymph nodes were removed from under his left arm. Surgeons also cut through shoulder muscles and nerves and removed two muscles, one behind his left shoulder and one that wrapped around his back.

After the surgery there was serious doubt that Littler would ever play golf again, much less competitive tournament golf. Yet within four months he had rebuilt his strength sufficiently to shoot a sixty-nine in a pro-am tournament. Then in October, 1972, Gene Littler tied for fifth in the Japanese Masters, shooting 281, and by 1973 he was again regularly competing on the US tour.

In awarding Littler the 1973 Bob Jones Award for distinguished sportsmanship in golf, the United States Golf Association highlighted his quiet courage and the fine example he had set for other golfers who have suffered disabilities. The distinguished American golfing body also commended the unfailing sportsmanship and dignity Littler had displayed throughout his playing career. No man has more richly deserved such recognition.

In 1973, twenty-five of Littler's contemporaries on the US pro tour named him as one of the finest swingers in the game in an article in *Golf Digest* magazine. I heartily concur with that vote.

Never a flamboyant golfer, he has meshed his personal and playing styles into a model of consistency – the name of the game when you are playing for your living. I believe he will continue as a model for even his fellow tournament professionals as long as he goes on playing.

Ken Bowden

1

2

3

Analysis

I first experienced American golf during the winter tour of 1955, and I well remember the impact Gene Littler was then making on the scene with his youth, strength and marvellously economical and efficient action. But after some initial successes, he suddenly entered into a slump that troubled him for at least two or three years. The reason was that his swing became very flat, and I think it was only in working himself out of this phase that Gene really learned to

play the game, and thus acquired the knowledge that is essential to become a consistent winner. Many top golfers have had to go through what Littler went through then, which is a transition from an instinctive to a reasoned and self-analytical approach to the game.

I believe a key to Littler's re-emergence as a fine player in the early 1960s was the weakening of his left-hand grip, which helped him to swing his arms on a more upright plane while still making a relatively

4

5

6

flat shoulder turn. Previously he had suffered from a tendency – common to strong grippers – to swing his arms around his body, in a very flat plane too closely related to his shoulder turn. This resulted in a destructive hook.

Littler's action today is one I'd recommend in its entirety to any player seeking a model of excellence. He is beautifully orthodox all the way from his address position (frame 1) to the end of what is generally accepted to be the perfect follow-through position.

Frame 5 is a particularly important picture for the golfer who slices or fails to deliver the club solidly into the back of the ball. You see clearly here that the plane of Littler's shoulder turn is flatter than that of his arm-swing. This is common to the majority of great players, but is an element of golf technique that is generally missed – or misinterpreted – by theorists in discussions of swing plane.

7   8   9

At the top (frame 6) Littler is beautifully set to deliver the clubhead powerfully and accurately into the back of the ball – arms, hands, head and clubhead all perfectly positioned.

As the hips unwind in the downswing, it is very noticeable (frames 7 and 8) how the left arm leads the club, leaving the shoulders behind, and how the right side stays 'under' the left side (frames 8 and 9). Notice, too, how at impact (frame 10) the club is approaching from immediately behind the ball – surely the number one objective in any game where we are trying to propel the ball forward.

Frame 11 shows a classical end of swing position – if you finish like this you are almost certain to have hit a fine shot.

John Jacobs

10

11

12

Gary Player

Unequalled dedication

Profile

Few golfers merit super-star status in all corners of the world, but Gary Player is certainly such a champion. The 37-year-old South African has won almost everything that matters, not only in his homeland, but in Britain, America, Australia, Japan and many other countries. One of the toughest competitors ever seen in any sport, Player shows no signs of losing his desire for gold and glory. Each year as he returns to the US tour, he restates his ambition of being the greatest golfer who ever lived.

Player is one of only four men to have won all four major championships (Gene Sarazen, Ben Hogan and Jack Nicklaus are the others). He took the British Open in 1959 and 1968, the US Masters in 1961, the US Open in 1965 and the US PGA Championship in 1962 and 1972. Since he started trekking to the US in 1955, Player has won fifteen American tournaments. During 1972 he played in only fifteen tournaments in the US, less than any of the top fifty moneywinners, but won two titles and ranked seventh in earnings with $120 720 – an average take of $7869 per tournament. It is this consistency of form that had put Player fourth in the US all-time moneywinners list, with $939 607, by the end of 1972.

Only 5′ 8″ and 11½ stone, Player is famous for his commitment to physical fitness. He exercises extensively and regularly, the regime including massive doses of weight-lifting and jogging, and he is also hyper diet-conscious. The approach – unusual among top golfers – certainly works for him. Despite his lack of inches and poundage, Player is as long from the tee as all but the monster hitters. And he is usually less tired at the end of a round than most of the fans who've sat in the stands watching all day.

All his life Player has been a glutton for practice, and it has certainly paid off. He was not gifted at the outset with a good natural swing, and is perhaps the supreme example of the fact that a super golf game can be manufactured, given enough willpower and energy.

Player possesses a great deal of moral as well as physical courage. A few years back, his life was frequently threatened by American militants opposed to the racial policies of South Africa, making his US appearances a test of nerve as well as golfing skill. Protesting his lack of influence on his country's policies, Player responded by inviting the black American golfer, Lee Elder, to play with him in what twice has turned out to be a highly successful series of exhibition matches in South Africa.

Even under the unique strain of having to be guarded by police on the golf course, Player never lost his temper nor his game. Today, although those pressures seem to have relented, Gary has cut back his US playing schedule somewhat, trying to devote more time to his large family and to his beloved ranch-type farm in South Africa. But to the tournaments he plays, he still brings a game and a will to win as strong as that of any golfer on the course.

Ken Bowden

1   2   3

Analysis

Gary Player has been a personal friend of mine for nearly twenty years, and I shall never cease to be amazed at what he has achieved. When Gary first came to Britain as a relatively poor boy in his teens, no one watching him swing could possibly have predicted his later achievements. He had an extremely flat action that required him to make a mass of ungainly compensations and counter-compensations, and a controlled draw was just about the only shot in his armoury.

But what he had then, as he still has today, was complete dedication to high ideals, plus the fiercest competitive temperament I've ever encountered. The first result was the development, in a remarkably short time, of an extremely effective and repetitive golf swing. The second was the development of great physical power through intensive exercise, brought on by his realisation that for a small man to be able to compete with the Palmers and Nicklauses, he must acquire much more than the normal degree of muscular strength and conditioning. Gary today is probably the strongest golfer pound-for-

4   5   6

·pound in the history of the game, but even so his achievements across the world are staggering for so small a fellow.

At address (frame 1) Player exhibits a grip that can best be described as anti-hook (bouts of hooking still occasionally plague him) and unusually rigid arms. This tense-looking arm set-up would be fatal for many lesser players, creating a rigidity that would carry over into other parts of the swing. But it does not seem to inhibit Gary's fluidity of movement – probably due to his extremely athletic and supple body.

As do many top golfers, during his backswing Gary turns his head slightly to his right (frame 4). This is a turn-promoting device that helps him to develop the width of arc (frames 3 through 5) so essential if he is to swing the clubhead into the back of the ball travelling at ground level through impact.

Frame 5 offers a wonderful illustration of the spring-like winding or coiling of the upper body, against the resistance of the lower body, by which top players generate such powerful leverage and, through that, clubhead speed. Note the huge amount of shoulder turn in

7
8
9

relation to the limited hip turn and the absence of any lift or give in the left foot.

Player 'sets' the club beautifully at the top, on a plane and in a direction that will allow him to deliver it into the back of the ball with maximum natural 'release'. If we were looking down the line of the shot we would see that the clubshaft parallels the target line – the perfect angle for uncontrived delivery of club to ball on the down-and through-swing. Note also that the clubface is open – toe pointing groundward – allowing Player plenty of room for hand and wrist action in the hitting area. There is no 'block' in this swing!

Frames 6 and 7 superbly illustrate how the top golfers initiate the downswing with the left side – the legs unwinding the left hip by shuttling towards the target; the unwinding hips pulling the left arm down; the unwinding left arm leading the club handle into the hitting area.

Golfers who suffer from the 'late-hit' syndrome should study what occurs in Player's swing between frames 8 and 10. His hips are continuing to turn and clear, of course, but apart from that the accent

24

10   11   12

here is not on body movement, *but on swinging arms and releasing wrists*, so that the clubhead is delivered into the *very back* of the ball.

Remember, you must clear your hips to make room for your arms to move past your body, *but you must also swing your arms and unhinge your wrists* if you are to have any chance of hitting the back of the ball with the clubface square.

Frames 10 and 11 show Gary's shoulders working very much on a tilted or 'underneath' plane through impact. At times, when his hip clearance is slow, this tilted shoulder action has a blocking effect on his arm swing, which forces him to roll his wrists through impact, rather than as here (frame 11) after the ball is well on its way. It is when that happens that he usually begins to hit the ball too much from right to left, and enters one of his very rare slumps.

John Jacobs

Johnny Miller

Superb confidence

Profile

Every year in the USA, a new crop of youthful contenders bursts out of amateur golf on to the pro tour, full of strength and vigor and confidence, and visions of sweeping victories, world acclaim and huge piles of dollars. Most of these youngsters never fulfill their dreams and are quickly forgotten. But one who has dramatically worked his way in a relatively short time to a prominent and seemingly permanent place in the sun is Johnny Miller.

Winner of the 1964 US Junior championship, Johnny Miller first burst onto the national American scene in the 1966 US Open at San Francisco's Olympic Club, the course where he learned to play golf. The then 19-year-old college student, who already had fourteen years of golfing experience, surprised everyone but himself by finishing an impressive eighth in a field that included every major golfer then competing on the US circuit.

Since turning professional three years later, the tall, blond, ultra-boyish-looking Miller has continued to play with a quiet confidence and a shot-making finesse that belie his years. His first professional victory was the 1971 Southern Open, and he also tied for second in the US Masters that year. He managed to win $91 081 in 1971, a notable jump from the comfortable $50 391 he earned in 1970, his first full year on tour.

In 1972, Miller, a native of California and a devout member of the Mormon church, continued to pick up steam, winning the Heritage Classic, placing second in the Bing Crosby Pro-Am and the US PGA National Team Championship, and finishing a creditable seventh in the US Open. Overall in 1972, he finished in the money in twenty-five of the thirty tournaments he entered and took home $99 348, which placed him seventeenth in money winnings for that year.

If in 1972 Miller showed he could hold his own with the best that professional golf has to offer, in 1973 he became much more special than that to the man in the street by virtue of just one round in the US Open, played at the historic Oakmont Country Club in Pennsylvania. At the end of the third round, Johnny wasn't even in the running, having posted a depressing seventy-six on top of a seventy-one and a sixty-nine in the opening rounds. But on that final day Miller came out of nowhere to win the tournament with an incredible, almost flawless, record-breaking sixty-three – the lowest final round in any of golf's major championships, and regarded by many experts as one of the greatest rounds of golf in history.

Miller went on to finish second to Tom Weiskopf three weeks later in the British Open, and wound up the year by winning the individual trophy in the World Cup in Spain, as well as the team championship for America with Jack Nicklaus. At the end of 1973 he was ninth on the US money list with $127 833, and had amassed career earnings of $374 731.

A quiet, reflective, observant and articulate young man, who does everything but play golf left-handed, Johnny was introduced to golf by his father, who spared no end to develop his son's talent once it became clearly evident during his early 'teens.

Unlike many tournament professionals, Miller is an accomplished swing theoretician who enjoys teaching the game almost as much as playing it. His style is modelled on Jack Nicklaus, whom he idolizes, and Nicklaus has said on more than one occasion that he believes Miller to have one of the finest swings on tour.

Ken Bowden

1   2   3

Analysis

Johnny Miller achieved instant stardom with his final round 63 to win the US Open at Oakmont in 1973.

Miller had put together a number of solid performances prior to his sensational Oakmont victory, and those despite a golf swing containing, in my view, a very obvious flaw. For some years he fell into the trap of getting the club back with a rocking or tilting rather than a turning motion of his shoulders. In this type of action the club certainly stays close to the target line during the takeaway, but when the movement is overdone it inevitably leads to an excessive lifting of the right side later in the backswing. The result of this is a reciprocal lifting and stretching of the left side during the through-swing, which on occasion will prevent the hips from turning and clearing to allow the arms to swing past the body. And the result of that 'blocking' action is either a hook, if the golfer snaps his wrists to get the club through the ball; or a push if he restrains his hand action in an effort not to send the ball to the left.

Although Miller's swing is still very upright in terms of his arms and the club, I believe that in the past couple of years he has become aware of the disadvantages of over-tilting the shoulders and has

4   5   6

modified his action accordingly, thereby enabling himself to attack the ball more from an 'inside' direction. This more 'inside' approach of the club to the ball has facilitated better clearing of his left side in the hitting area, thus making room for his arms to swing through uninhibitedly on a wider arc to the target.

Looking now at frame 1, Miller's address position is 100 per cent orthodox, although I suspect that his back is more erect than it was a couple of years ago, which would automatically increase the amount he turns rather than tilts his shoulders during the backswing.

Frame 2 is interesting in that it shows the clubhead being left very slightly behind the hands during the takeaway. Without doubt this is a result of Miller's one-time excessive shoulder tilt – a common cause of 'dragging' the clubhead back behind the hands. A more important point to note here, however, is Miller's initial shoulder movement – now very much in a turning plane, although his arms and club are still swinging on a markedly upright path.

There is little to criticise in frame 3. The plane through Miller's shoulders is distinctly flatter than the plane of his left arm, which is a feature of most top golfers. And if the function of the backswing is to set both the body and the club in position to strike the ball forward – as I firmly believe it is – here you see a great backswing: the club pointing at the target on an upright plane, with the body

7   8   9

turned out of the way and fully coiled for a powerful through-swing.

Frame 4 beautifully illustrates how the good golfer leads the club to the ball from inside the target line by initiating the downswing with his legs and hips. You will note in frame 5 that, although the left hip is clearing, Miller's shoulders are still square to his target line through impact. He achieves this essential 'from the inside' attack on the ball, as all good players do, by swinging his arms freely in concert with his lower-body action.

From the position shown in frame 5, the natural reaction is to continue releasing the clubhead *through* the *back* of the ball with the hands, wrists and arms, and the very momentum of that release carries Miller to the position shown in frame 6. Here is the finish of a golfer who has hit the ball to the target, as opposed to hitting the club to the ball.

Frames 7, 8, 9, 10 and 11 further illustrate how Miller has retained an upright club arc, yet has been able to develop a more 'getting-out-of-the-way' body movement, in order to make room for the correct inside-to straight-to inside clubhead path through impact.

Frame 7 again illustrates an excellent set-up, plus a fine view of the typical modern professional tournament golfer's grip, char-

10   11   12

acterised by the back of left hand aiming very squarely and solidly at the target. Most weekend golfers holding the club thus would slice, but the tremendous clubhead release of the powerful modern tournament player necessitates such a grip to avoid hooking.

Frame 8 is a fine illustration of a full turn of the upper body against a resisting but resilient lower half. In frame 9 note again how the left side leads the downswing: the left heel here is already firmly replanted, the knees are working towards the target and the hips are beginning to turn – all this exerting a massive pull from the left shoulder via the arms to the club.

Frame 10 shows classical impact-zone form: hips well cleared to make room for the arms to swing past the body; weight on the left side; head behind the ball; eyes still on the ball's location; and the club fully released into the back of the ball by the hands, wrists and arms.

Johnny Miller today is a fine swinger of the club, blessed with excellent rhythm and tempo as well as sound mechanics. Since he also possesses the perfect temperament, his place among the superstars is assured.

John Jacobs

31

Julius Boros

Unflappable and so natural

Profile

Nobody makes the game of golf look easier than Julius Boros. Ambling through a round as if he hadn't a care in the world, this great golfer – now in his mid-fifties – has managed to win an impressive string of tournaments without even seeming to breathe hard.

Since turning professional in 1949 at the relatively advanced age of twenty-nine, Boros has given several generations of tournament hotshots a hard run for their money. Today he is able to combine play on the US senior circuit with an occasional stab at the pro tour – as witness his great play in the 1973 US Open – keeping his hand in to the tune of $25 774 in prize money in 1972. His many senior victories include the 1971 US PGA Seniors' Championship.

Among Boros' eighteen pro tour victories, his highlights were the 1952 and 1963 US Opens and the 1968 US PGA Championship – making him the oldest man ever to win one of the four major championships. He has played on two US Ryder Cup teams and was voted the US PGA Player of the Year in 1952 and 1963. The US tour's leading money winner in 1952 and 1955, he finished 1972 with a career earnings total of $889 863, placing him then fifth in the ranks of all-time money winners.

Although it sometimes seems that he'd prefer to be out fishing with his seven children, 'Jay,' as he's known on the US tour, takes his game seriously. His smooth, relaxed-looking swing is the result of a lifetime of practice, overcoming many of the same problems that face the weekend golfer. For instance, Boros has never considered putting a strong point in his game, but has had to work hard all his life to master it sufficiently to stay in the winners' circle. Today, when Boros strokes a putt – even a crucial one – he hesitates no more than he would to cross the street, but that seeming nonchalance has been hard won.

Most of his contemporaries on the US pro tour will tell you that the secret of Boros' casual-looking game is rhythm. He hits the ball a lot harder than appearances would indicate, but his rhythm is so flawless, his balance so good, that there is no appearance of force or effort. Boros is also one of the fastest players in tournament golf, never lingering over a shot no matter how important. He does all his checking and assessing on his way to the ball and, once there, is always ready to hit – before tension can begin to creep into his mind and muscles. This, many of his contemporaries believe, is another of his secrets.

Friendly and likeable, the man with no visible nerves has considered retiring from golf, but just never seems to get around to it. He currently hosts an American television show in which he shares his wide sporting and outdoor interests with the public, which has cut into his time for golf. But Julius Boros hasn't lost his touch yet, and as long as he retains it he can be expected to be unnerving his fellow pros with that casual but deadly game.

Ken Bowden

1   2   3

Analysis

I believe that Julius Boros' longevity, like Sam Snead's, stems from his relaxed and essentially *reactive* approach to the game. Boros has found a way to play that is so natural to him physically that he can swing instinctively rather than with the great conscious mental effort and physical deliberation that characterizes many of the younger tournament players. The result is that his swing has become immensely repetitive without the need for the perpetual nit-picking analysis

and fine tuning that plagues the more artificial player. Boros' ability around the greens stems from a first-class technique and an unflappable temperament, and this is to be seen nowhere more clearly than when he steps into a bunker.

The critical factor on all short shots around the green is the angle at which the clubhead approaches the ball. In sand it is absolutely vital that the club approaches the ball at an angle steep enough to

4   5   6

allow it to skid through the sand beneath the ball, without actually contacting the ball. Boros here exemplifies that technique.

Note in frames 2, 3 and 4 how the hands and wrists work the club-head up and down in a relatively narrow arc in order to hit down and through the sand beneath the ball (frame 5). This vital narrow arc is to be seen again from another angle in frames 8, 9 and 10.

For the clubhead to slide or skid through the sand, rather than bury itself in the sand, it must remain open through impact. Like most good trap players, Boros sets the clubface thus at address (frame 7), then maintains the open position through his hand and arm action up to and through impact. Frame 10 provides a clear illustration of the open angle at which the clubface will approach and skid through the sand beneath the ball (to be seen in frame 11).

In studying the frontal views of Boros, notice particularly how

7   8   9

little body action he uses compared to hand, wrist and arm action. A big body turn promotes a wide arc and thus a flat-bottomed approach of club to ball. This is exactly the opposite of what is required in sand, thus Boros' pronounced use of the hands and wrists to steepen the arc and ensure that he slides the clubface *beneath* the ball.

Incidentally, I am always astounded by the average golfer's attitude to bunkers. The great players know they are going to get in sand, and therefore regularly practice getting out of it. The average golfer seems to assume that he'll never get in bunkers, and thus rarely practices from them. The result is usually ineptitude any time such a player enters sand.

John Jacobs

36

10

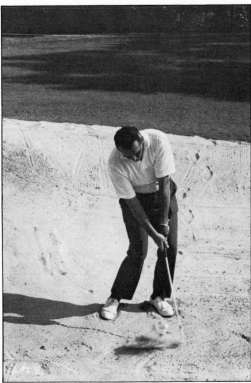

11

12

LeeTrevino

A unique swing

Profile

Probably no single figure has injected more fun and spirit into modern professional tournament golf than Lee Trevino. 'Supermex', as he's known to all US golfers, has captivated galleries all over the world in recent years by combining spectacular play with a casual, happy-go-lucky manner, and an inexhaustible fund of humorous observations and wisecracks for his fellow pros and his enormous galleries. At his most effervescent, he has been known to start a quip at address, get to the middle of it at the top of his backswing, and deliver the punch-line at impact. Not since Jimmy Demaret has the game had so loquacious a character.

Trevino's meteoric rise in golf is a genuine rags-to-riches story. The fourth golfer to join the sport's million dollar winners' circle (in early 1973), Trevino began life as a poor boy in Texas, developing his game while serving with the US Marines, and perfected it on driving ranges and public courses in his pre-tournament 'hustling' days. Some of his best stories are about playing hard-headed – and hard-hitting-Texans for more money than he possessed.

Trevino first hit the headlines in 1968, by being the first golfer in history to break seventy in all four rounds of the US Open and thereby beating Jack Nicklaus for the title by four shots. The previous year he had finished sixth in the US Open at his first try, but it was his Open victory that see Lee flying. Five years later he had won sixteen tournaments, including another US Open and two British Opens, played on two winning US World Cup teams (1969 and 1971), been US PGA Player of the Year (1971), and won the Vardon Trophy for best scoring average in the US three straight years (1970–72) – plus, of course, accumulating more than a million dollars in prize money. Of all his feats during that period, perhaps his most sensational was victory in the US, Canadian and British Opens within the space of a four-week period.

Still only thirty-four years old, Trevino shows few signs of slowing down. He has a reputation for enjoying the money he's earning, and the way it is spent is a source of many of his famous wisecracks, although his predilection for cold beer and late nights has been tempered of late by his hectic playing and business schedule.

Sometimes erratic on the course, Lee on his game is as good a golfer as anyone in the world, and he has been known to just get up and go home on those days when he is clearly not on his stick. Very infrequently, however, is he anything but light-hearted on the surface. In the 1971 US Open playoff at Merion, for example, he startled opponent Jack Nicklaus and just about everyone else by throwing a rubber snake at Jack as they waited to tee off. At the British Open in 1971, while waiting at the sixth tee at Royal Birkdale, he had the gallery in fits with his animated descriptions of cricket, seen the previous day on TV.

However, anyone who plays as well and wins as much as Trevino does has to take the game extremely seriously, and no one in modern golf thinks more about his technique or practices more assiduously (usually away from the actual tournament site). He has a real affection for his fans, and a strong sense of responsibility to the US tournament sponsors. In 1972 he played in thirty-one US tournaments, compared with Jack Nicklaus's nineteen and Arnold Palmer's twenty-two. His unorthodox-looking swing is frequently dissected by US analysts, but whatever it lacks in classical beauty it more than makes up for in effectiveness on the course. Jack Nicklaus, for example, regards him as one of the finest shot-makers who ever lived, and his most serious rival for major honours.

In the often humourless quest for the big stakes of professional golf, Lee Trevino provides a much-appreciated breath of fresh air.

Ken Bowden

1   2.   3

Analysis

A major factor behind the world-wide golf boom is, I'm sure, the quality of the people who have dominated the game in recent years, and to my mind Lee Trevino is right up there alongside Arnold Palmer, Jack Nicklaus, Gary Player and Billy Casper as a man of immense character and integrity. Despite his rugged early struggles, he has no chips on his shoulder, and his humour is spontaneous and fresh and full of genuine wry wit and an obvious liking for people. Very few top professional sportsmen, in my experience, can always

see the funny side of things, especially when they are losing. Trevino usually can, which is most refreshing and likeable.

I believe Lee's greatest asset as a golfer is his ability to remain the same person under tremendous strain, which is a quality that may have grown out of his rugged early life and the need to rely entirely on his own wits and skills simply to put food in his stomach. Certainly his intense – but usually well-disguised – competitiveness must derive from those hard years of struggle and frustration.

Technically, Trevino is a one-thousand per cent better golfer than he often looks to the style-conscious amateur. He has a fine

4

5

6

brain and a very sound and deep knowledge of his own game, acquired through many years of self-analysis, experiment and relentless practice. In essence, his method is that of the golfer who hooked everything so badly for so long that everything he now does is a defence against the violent right-to-left shot. Of all those defences, setting up way left of target is his prime bastion against the once disastrous hook.

Early in 1973 I listened with great interest to Lee talking about his game at a tournament in Miami, Florida. He said that he thinks his greatest strength is that he is able to sense the position of the club-head throughout the swing. If golf is ball control – and I believe very firmly that it is – then this is a priceless asset, because it is the key to flighting the ball high, low, left and right. And there is certainly no more precise manoeuvrer of the ball in golf today than this like-able Mexican-American.

In common with most top tournament golfers, Trevino rarely tries to hit the ball dead straight. His long shots are predominantly played with a slight fade (the ultimate anti-hook medicine), whereas many of his short-iron shots come into the flag slightly from the right.

Deliberate and finely-controlled changes in clubface delivery are

7   8   9

partly responsible for this in Lee's case – for example, his clubface is much less shut at the top of the swing with a short-iron than with a wooden club. But there is also a ballistical factor involved here which amateur golfers would do well to understand, the crux of which is that the straighter-faced the club, the easier it is to fade the ball, this becoming virtually impossible with the heavily lofted clubs.

It is apparent in frame 1 how much Lee's left side is pulled back (or opened) from the target line. I believe that this set-up has derived over a period of time from his unusually strong right-hand grip (frame 1). Aiming well left of target facilitates fast body clearance in the downswing, which in turn helps to delay wrist-rolling through impact. With so strong a grip, Trevino must always guard against any move – like wrist-rolling – that would further close the clubface through the ball.

Trevino has a particularly wide one-piece takeaway (frames 2 and 3), and a magnificently full shoulder turn at the top of the swing (frame 5). Both are essential to enable a man of his short stature to deliver the club powerfully into the back of the ball at ground level, and are key factors in his ability to drive such long distances, despite a very delayed or 'blocked' release of his hands and wrists

10   11   12

(necessary to prevent further closing of an already shut clubface).

Frames 6 through 9 illustrate that, although Trevino uses his legs and hips to a pronounced degree on the downswing, like all great players he combines this lower-body movement with a powerful swing of the arms. If he were to leave out his arm action, there would be no way he could deliver the club solidly into the back of the ball.

You will note in frame 9 that, as the clubhead is finally delivered to the ball, the wrists have still not been fully released and that the back of Lee's left hand is looking to the right of his target. This is, in effect, a 'blocking' action, and is common to all strong-gripping, flat-swinging, shut-faced golfers. It goes with the lateral leg slide and hip turn that is also a pronounced feature of Lee's swing, and is responsible for his unusually deep right-arm extension and 'underneath' shoulder action into the follow-through (frames 10 and 11).

John Jacobs

43

Arnold Palmer

Still the most thrilling
to watch

Profile

There's nothing to say about Arnold Palmer that hasn't been said ten thousand times before. Forever supported by 'Arnie's Army,' he can legitimately be given much of the credit for bringing golf its current massive popularity across the globe. And although he may not be dominating the US tour these days, a great mass of Americans still wait patiently in the wings to roar him to victory, as they did with wild abandon in the 1973 Bob Hope Desert Classic.

The 44-year-old Palmer has had his troubles in the past few years, not least with his eyesight, but the Hope result proved what he's always saying – that he isn't through yet. Since joining the US tour in 1955, Arnold has won fifty-seven tournaments, placing him behind only Sam Snead as the world's most prolific winner. Palmer's victories include the Masters in 1958, 1960, 1962 and 1964, the 1960 US Open, and the 1961 and 1962 British Opens. He still burns to win the PGA Championship, and the famous Palmer charge may yet make that ambition a reality.

Beyond his tournament wins Arnie has, of course, also piled up an endless list of mosts and bests. He won the US Vardon Trophy for lowest scoring average four times – in 1961, 1962, 1964 and 1967. His career earnings, through 1972, totalled $1 580 880, second only to Jack Nicklaus. He has been on six winning World Cup teams for the United States, and was US PGA Player of the Year in 1960 and 1962.

As the most famous golfer in history, Palmer has probably done more than any other individual to build the game's image and stature in his own country and many others – including Britain, where he almost single-handedly put the Open back on the map in the early '60s. Among formal tributes to his contribution to golf have been the United States Golf Association's Bobby Jones Award for distinguished sportsmanship, and the Golf Writers Association of America's Richardson Award for outstanding contributions to the game. In 1970, the Associated Press selected him as the Outstanding Athlete of the Decade.

Palmer's massive reputation and popularity have hardly been dented by his golfing problems in recent years, although they have been an endless topic of discussion among his fellow pros, the press, and amateur and professional watchers of the game around the world. Once unquestionably the game's bravest and finest putter, he has been increasingly troubled by his putting, and has experimented with scores of variations on that famous knock-kneed, wristy theme. None seem to have worked more than temporarily, but, despite his troubles, Palmer wound up 1972 as 25th in the PGA money list, with earnings of $84 181. He got off to a better start in 1973, collecting one victory and $41 777 by mid-April, and he intends for there to be more.

Ken Bowden

1   2   3

Analysis

I have always been and I'm sure always will be a member of 'Arnie's Army'. Of all the golfers I've ever seen, given a free choice to go out and watch one tomorrow I'd choose Palmer. His aggressiveness, his courage, his power, his spontaneity and his humanity never lose their appeal, even when he is not in contention – which happily he still often is.

I'm sure a lot of people who follow golf do not realise – or have forgotten – what a fantastic putter Arnold was during his golden

years from the mid 'fifties through the early 'sixties. One had the impression in those days that wherever the ball was on the green, he thought he could hole it out. And, of course, very often he did.

As a striker of the long shots at that time, Palmer varied between brilliance and wild inaccuracy. His talent was always immense, but frequently – and this was his charm – his sheer aggressiveness, his determination to 'charge' the course, cost him control. He just could not play conservatively, and on many occasions it was his putting that saved the day.

4   5   6

Arnold's game was forged around the principle of giving the ball the healthiest possible wallop, and to facilitate this he instinctively learned to make a big turn going back and an equally uninhibited turn going through. This led him into a pronouncedly flat swing plane, and, early in his career, a strongish grip, that often produced a thundering hook. Pretty soon he realised he was going to have to modify his grip to lessen his tendency to deliver the clubface to the ball in a closed position. Gradually over the years he has also – through increasing technical knowledge, I'm sure – developed a more upright arm-swing arc and thus a more upright clubhead path, without inhibiting his natural full shoulder turn. The result is that he is now one of the finest and most consistent strikers of the ball the game has ever seen – I personally would nominate him as the finest driver of the ball in the world at this moment.

But, alas, along with this gain in long-shot control, he seems to have lost that wonderful ability he had at his peak to literally *ram* the ball into the hole on the greens.

I am a believer that there are only so many good fights in all of us,

7   8   9

and that the business of holing out from two to five feet year after year must eventually exhaust most men's nerves. But I can't help feeling that Arnold would be better off as a tournament golfer if only he had a deep enough interest outside the game to be able to get right away from it periodically. I understand that such restorative periods are often planned, but that within a very short time he is back to manipulating golf clubs or hitting practice shots. Certainly no man has ever loved the game more, but it really is possible to try too hard, and I suspect he may often do just that.

In frames 1 and 2, Arnold exhibits the perfect address position and a perfect takeaway, exemplified by the one-piece unit of the left arm and club shaft – no independent hand and wrist action here.

Frame 3 offers a clue to the source of Palmer's great power, in that his shoulders have turned through more than 45 degrees before the club has reached much more than a horizontal position. Most average golfers at this point in the swing would have turned their shoulders less but would have raised the club higher with their hands and arms.

The full extent of Arnold's shoulder turn is to be seen in frame 5,

10   11   12

but notice, too, the comparatively upright plane of his arms. At one time Arnold's arm plane matched his shoulder plane, creating a very flat action both sides of the ball and, often, causing inaccuracy.

Frames 6 through 10 show the downswing action common to all great modern golfers: an unwinding and clearing of the lower body coordinated with a downward swing of the arms, leading to an 'in-time' release of the club through the hands and wrists that delivers the clubhead fast and solidly into the back of the ball at ground level.

In Palmer's case, as with other very powerful hitters, the massive momentum of the release forces the hands to roll over fairly early in the follow-through (frame 11), but the ball by now is well on its way.

Note throughout the sequence Arnie's wonderfully steady head. There is no better 'looker at the ball' in golf, and it is a major key to his success.

John Jacobs

Tom Weiskopf

A handsome swinger

Profile

Tom Weiskopf, the 1973 British Open Champion, presents a fascinating example of the critical importance of the mind, or psyche, in golf.

'Big T', as his friends call him in the States, joined the US tour in 1965, and immediately demonstrated a massive natural talent for golf. He hit the ball farther than Jack Nicklaus, with a more fluent-looking and, at times, a seemingly flawless swing. He was young, strong and athletic. He had the incentive of being unsponsored – how he ate depended on how he played. There was hardly a golf shot he could not play, at least on the practice tee. And yet Weiskopf did not excel. It took him three years to win his first tournament, and by the end of 1972 he had won only five US tour events. Worse yet, he had developed a reputation among press and fans for surliness and bad temper – the latter often exemplified by his tempestuous reactions to what he regarded as bad shots.

Signs of a new Weiskopf first became visible in 1972, when he won the Jackie Gleason Inverarry Classic in Florida, finished second in the Masters, won the Piccadilly World Match-play Championship, and retained the club in his hand even after bad shots right through the year, to amass \$129 442 and finish sixth on the US prize money list.

But the real break-through came in 1973, and was, Tom believes, largely the result of some deep reappraising of his life caused by the death of his father early that year. Weiskopf had always recognized his own huge talent for golf – in fact, his temper tantrums were largely caused by his annoyance at himself for not making the most of it. The death of his father gave him for the first time a burning resolve to use that talent to the full. The immediate result was three victories out of four consecutive starts in the US in the spring and early summer of 1973, followed by a peerless win, leading from start to finish, in the British Open at Troon in July – his first major championship.

Married to a former state beauty queen, and the father of two young children, Weiskopf at thirty-one seems at last to have found himself. Beyond his superb golf in Scotland, Tom's unfailing good humour and friendliness endeared him to both the press and the public at Troon, and this new image has caused a similar quick upsurge in his popularity in the US.

Many of Weiskopf's contemporaries on the American tour believe that, now he has put a 'head' on top of his superb swing, there is a strong chance he could move into the super-star class. That Tom will certainly be trying is implicit in his statement at Troon: 'My goal now is to win more major championships than Jack Nicklaus.'

Ken Bowden

1   2   3

Analysis

Tom Wieskopf today is probably the finest striker of a golf ball in the world, but it wasn't always that way. In addition to his temperamental problems, for a long time this handsome man had a swing that flattered to deceive, by which I mean it was not quite as good as it looked.

In the US, Weiskopf has been regarded by close golf followers as the heir-apparent to Jack Nicklaus ever since he joined the pro tour nine years ago. His failure to match Jack constantly puzzled even his fellow players. I recall Tony Jacklin remarking to me one day that he couldn't understand why his friend Weiskopf 'didn't win everything'.

I gave Tony at that time my opinion that Tom, like so many other young American players, had fallen into the trap of trying to swing the club too much on a straight line. The result was too much shoulder tilt on the backswing, leading to periodic disastrously wild shots, leading in turn to discouragement or loss of temper on Tom's part.

Whether Weiskopf has changed his shoulder plane consciously or unconsciously, I don't know, but without doubt it has flattened in

52

4   5   6

the last two years. The result is not only a swing that delights the eye, but one that is now extremely sound and functional in every technical aspect.

Weiskopf is self-admittedly a 'natural' rather than a manufactured golfer, by which he means that he has always swung instinctively rather than in a studied mechanical manner. It is this freedom from artifice that gives his swing such grace and freedom and visual appeal. But the real key to his superb striking is, in my view, his superb hand-eye coordination – a priceless asset also to Jack Nicklaus. Very few people in the world are gifted with the coordination necessary to deliver the clubhead solidly into the back of the ball time and time again while swinging on the massive arcs characteristic of Weiskopf and Nicklaus.

In frame 1 Weiskopf exemplifies the modern 'power' set-up: feet firmly planted and knees springily flexed, all ready for the lower body to resist the turning of the upper body, and thus create the massive

53

7   8   9

torque that is the source of his huge drives. Note how the head and upper body are set *behind* the ball – essential to be able to drive it *forward*.

Weiskopf swings the club back with his arms in command (frames 2 and 3), the arms pulling the shoulders into a superbly coiled top of the backswing position (frames 4 and 5). Great strength and suppleness are needed to coil the upper body and swing the arms as high as Weiskopf does, without lifting the left heel or allowing more than a few degrees of hip turn.

You will see few better examples of 'leading the downswing with the legs' than Weiskopf illustrates here (frame 6). But, to understand what the word 'release' means, compare the location of the clubhead in frames 6 and 7, in relation to the degree of lower-body movement that has occurred between these two pictures. All that has happened down below has been in increase in the turning of the hips to the left, but *the clubhead has moved from behind Weiskopf's head to within three feet of the ball*. This is the bit the deliberate 'late-hitters' leave out.

54

10   11   12

Weiskopf continues to drive with his legs right through impact, but the clubhead is released in plenty of time by his arms and hands, so that it travels low and solidly through the *back* of the ball (frames 7 and 8).

Few golfers I've seen stay more 'behind' the ball, or retain as steady a head position as deep into the follow-through as does Weiskopf (frames 9 and 10). Again this demands great strength and suppleness, as well as a smooth clearance of the left hip to make way for the arms to swing freely past the body (frame 9).

Tall men generally swing into a full follow-through, but Tom's finish is among the fullest and most majestic I have ever seen. A fitting finale to a fabulous golf swing.

John Jacobs

55

Tony Jacklin

British Open Champion '69
US Open Champion '70

Profile

Tony Jacklin, the first golfing hero Britain has had since Henry Cotton to be recognized by the man in the street all over the world, hardly needs introduction here. When he won the British Open in 1969, he was the first Briton to do so in eighteen years. When he won the United States Open in 1970 he was the first of his countrymen to accomplish that feat in 50 years. He's been a national sports hero at home now for five years, and shows every sign of remaining a head-line-maker wherever golf is played for many more years.

'Jacko,' still only twenty-nine, chose golf as his profession at a very early age. Introduced to the game as a caddie when he was eleven, Tony joined his father's golf club at the age of thirteen, working at various odd jobs in order to pay the fee. By the time he was sixteen he had left school and turned professional. There was never any doubt in his mind that golf would be his career, no matter what obstacles he had to overcome – and there were plenty in the early years, including an acute shortage of cash.

Jacklin has played all over the world since he first joined the British circuit in 1963, making friends and winning titles in South Africa, North and South America, Australia, New Zealand, the Far East and on the Continent of Europe. He has also represented Britain in the 1966 World Cup and the 1967, 1969 and 1971 Ryder Cup teams.

Tony's rise to the top has been fast, and not at all hindered by his driving ambition to become one of the best players in the world. After his first major British win, the Pringle in 1967, he started to eye the lucrative and prestigious US PGA tour. His first win there was the Jacksonville Open in 1968, and he subsequently captured the 1970 US Open and 1972 Jacksonville Open. Although he played only 20 tournaments in the United States in 1972, Jacklin took home $65 976 in prize money, placing him thirty-fifth on the money list.

Jacklin's golfing prowess has brought him much personal reward, as well as a place in the record books and in the hearts of his people. After he won the British Open in 1969, the Queen awarded him the OBE. He is also the proud owner of a magnificent country home in the Cotswolds and a Rolls Royce – quite a step for a boy who delivered newspapers to pay for his golf less than two decades ago.

In 1973, after his first real slump on the world circuit, Jacklin decided to confine most of his endeavours to Europe, a decision influenced by his dislike of being away from his family, plus the fast growth of prize-money and other profit opportunities in the UK and on the Continent. At the time of writing there were strong signs that his decision would quickly have a rejuvenating effect on his game. Certainly many American fans, who like Jacklin's looks and accent as much as his game, hope that he returns to conquer again in the USA.

Ken Bowden

1

2

3

Analysis

Not since Henry Cotton has Britain produced a golfer of Tony Jacklin's stature, and his influence on British – even European – golf has been vast, and all for the good. Indeed, much of the recent growth of the professional tournament game in Europe is directly or indirectly due to Jacklin, as I'm sure most of his fellow professionals have come to recognize.

Like all great players, Tony's success derives as much from dedica-

tion and tenacity as it does from technical excellence. Indeed, it is my belief that both his major championship victories were more the result of his temperament than his technique – and I say this without in any way intending to belittle his enormous talent for golf.

As a youngster Tony fell into the common fault of addressing the ball with his shoulders too open – aligned left of target. From that open-shouldered position, to avoid swinging outside the target line,

4   5   6

he was forced on the backswing to turn too obliquely away from the ball, which led to a rather flat swing plane and an overworking of the shoulders in the downswing.

As he matured, Tony learned one of the fundamental truths of golf, which is that if you do not aim and set-up correctly you give yourself a very slim chance of hitting the ball solidly and consistently accurately. The result eventually was his adoption of a square address alignment, which promoted a more upright arm swing in unison with a free, full shoulder turn. When he uses this swing – and he still tends occasionally to fall back into old habits – Jacklin is one of the finest strikers of the ball in the world.

Even when using his old swing Tony was often able to score well due to a superb short game allied to a fierce competitive spirit. Whether he is as fierce a competitor today as he was five years ago is open

7   8   9

to question, but it is my belief that the urge to be the best in the world will return, and that Jacklin will remain a force on the international golfing scene for many years to come.

At address (frame 1) Tony is 100 per cent orthodox, and an excellent model for every weekend golfer. He takes the club back with a perfect combination of shoulder turn and free arm swing, and I have rarely seen a better example of a golfer resiliently resist-ing the upper body turn with the lower half of the body (frame 3).

Frame 5 illustrates an admirable top-of-the-backswing position, although one could certainly not call his swing plane on this occasion upright. It is when Tony becomes flatter than this that his clubface tends to become too closed and he has to fight the left side of the course.

You will rarely see a better example of how the legs and hips should

initiate and lead the downswing than in frames 6 through 10, *but note also in these pictures how the arms have swung the club in unison with the lower-body action*, and how the hands and wrists release the clubhead into the back of the ball travelling low to the ground in frames 9 and 10.

The rather exaggerated leg-action Tony exhibits in frames 11 and 12 is an anti-hook measure often seen in golfers whose natural tendency to bring the ball in from the right sometimes gets out of hand.

Overall a very fine, compact and powerful swing.

John Jacobs

Billy Casper

A master of the short game

Profile

The 1970s and Billy Casper haven't quite got together yet, but the 42-year-old one-time super-star isn't prepared to just sit back and rest on his laurels. Finishing forty-first in money earnings for 1972, with no victories for the year, Casper has had to struggle mightily against a prolonged slump and with allergies which have prevented him from playing in some parts of the US.

A slow climber to the top ranks, Casper blossomed during the sixties, shedding his golfing problems along with a substantial amount of weight. A quiet, unpretentious and devout man, he has always let his clubs speak for his golf, but has used his fame and his voice increasingly in recent years as a missionary for the Mormon church, in partnership with his wife, Shirley.

Casper's tournament wins have included the 1970 Masters, the 1959 and 1966 US Open, and the 1969 Alcan Golfer of the Year tournament. Bill captured the US Vardon Trophy for lowest scoring average in 1960, 1963, 1965, 1966 and 1968, and was US PGA Player of the Year in 1966, 1968 and 1970.

A fellow who enjoys travel, Casper has played on five US Ryder Cup teams and in tournaments in every corner of the globe. His victories include the 1958 and 1959 Brazilian Open and the 1967 Canadian Open. In recent years, he has been a frequent visitor to and golf instructor for King Hassan of Morocco. But Casper is essentially a homebody and a family man, never happier than when relaxing in his San Diego, California, home with his wife and seven children (four of whom are adopted).

Casper is a cautious and conservative golfer, with a consistent but unspectacular long game and, at his best, a fabulous short game and putting stroke. Perhaps these talents have never been more in evidence than during his victory over Arnold Palmer in the 1966 US Open. Seven strokes behind Arnold as they entered the fourth round, Casper caught up with Palmer then defeated him in an eighteen-hole play-off. The victory won him world headlines, and, although he doesn't show his hunger on the surface, he'd like to win some more of them.

Ken Bowden

1   2   3

Analysis

As a young golfer Billy Casper fought a disastrous hook, and in fact only began to win on the US tour after learning to fade the ball. From that point in his career he has worked gradually back to a point where he now generally prefers to draw the ball gently from right to left. Such an evolutionary process has been common to many top golfers, Ben Hogan among them.

As I've stressed frequently in this and other books, temperament certainly plays as big a part in golf as technique, and in this area Casper has always been a champion. Of all his temperamental qualities perhaps his greatest is the ability to remain truly calm under pressure – he has often seemed to me, when at the centre of frenzied action, to·be the calmest person present.

Another factor behind Bill's richly deserved success has been a magnificent short game – a touch comparable, at its best, with the incomparable Bobby Locke's. Casper is also a superb chipper, pitcher and bunker player, but I believe his greatest single asset has

4   5   6

been his ability to hole out the difficult short putt under maximum pressure (we look at his putting method on page 68).

Yet another factor behind Casper's success is the economy of effort deriving from his non-histrionic approach to the game. Bill leaves the practice tee as soon as he has found his groove; he quietly plans his shots as he approaches the ball, then dispatches them speedily and without fuss; he plays for score, not effect; he maintains as consistent and calm a pace on the course as he does off it. These things add up in so frenetic an arena as the US pro tour.

Turning to Casper's technique, the first interesting point is his grip (frame 1). It is much stronger – hands turned more to the right – than that of most top golfers. Casper obviates the tendency to hook normally produced by this type of grip by swinging the club on a particularly upright plane, which causes the clubface to stay very 'square' to the target line on the takeaway (frame 2).

Again because of his strong grip and closed clubface (frame 4), Bill must cock his wrists very fully, even to the point of cupping his left wrist at the top of the swing (frame 5). Without this full wrist

65

7   8   9

cocking, he would be hard pressed to lead into the ball with his hands ahead of the clubface at impact, and would be prone to deliver the clubface to the ball in a closed alignment.

Like all shut-faced swingers, Casper's left side is very dominant in the downswing: notice his pronounced lateral leg and hip action in frames 6–9. This strong lateral leg-hip action, combined with his full wrist-cock, causes his hands to reach a position opposite to the ball before the clubhead is applied (frame 9). The strength of Casper's grip is one factor necessitating this very late release of the

wrists – if he uncocked earlier he would deliver the clubface to the ball in a closed position. But this is an individualistic way to play golf – and is certainly not medicine for most weekend golfers.

Frames 11 and 12, when related to frames 4 and 5, illustrate how pronouncedly 'up and under' and 'down and under' Casper swings. He perfectly exemplifies what I call the 'straight-line' concept of swing, as opposed to the more rotary pattern of a Sam Snead.

66

10   11   12

Casper's putting stroke, like his full swing, is immensely effective but definitely idiosyncratic.

Bill starts (frame 1) from an ideal and an orthodox position: eyes over ball; weight solidly planted; body comfortably balanced and square to target line; hands close to body and ball close to feet; putter shaft upright; reverse overlap grip with the back of the left hand and the palm of the right looking squarely at the target. It is in

his control of the clubface, and the resultant path of the stroke, that Casper departs from the norm.

In my observation, on putts of any length the great majority of fine putters tend to swing the club back slightly inside the target line, then return it straight through the ball along the target line at impact. This type of action promotes keeping the putterhead close to the ground throughout the stroke, engendering a level approach of club

4   5   6

to ball and thus a flush, solid hit. Casper takes the putter head straight back from the ball on an extension of the target line (frames 2 and 8), which causes it to rise quickly from the ground on a pronouncedly upward path (particularly noticeable in frame 3). At the same time, Bill holds the face of the putter absolutely square to his target line, which gives the impression (frames 3 and 9) that he is actually closing or hooding the club. In returning the putterhead to and through the ball, again Casper holds the clubface very square to his target line, giving the impression (frames 6 and 11) that he is opening it through the ball.

In actual fact, there is no closing or opening of the club during the stroke, but simply a consistent squareness of the putter face to the target line that produces a visual impression of rotation. Overall, the action is very comparable to that of a pendulum, which is arguably

7

8

9

the ideal kind of putting stroke in that it allows no deviation of the striking implement from the target line.

However, in actual fact Casper's method of putting is one I would recommend only to a golfer who could perform it in a natural rather than a contrived manner. What I would recommend to *all* golfers is the acceleration of the clubhead *through the ball* that is a feature of Bill's firm, positive stroke. And I would also recommend his calm, collected, controlled attitude to the game of golf at large, it being an inescapable fact that holing a four-foot putt when it matters is every bit as much a test of temperament as of technique.

John Jacobs

1

2

3

Sam Snead

The most natural golfer
of them all

Profile

If it's true that 'you're only as old as you feel,' then Sam Snead must feel about twenty-five. This 62-year-old golfing phenomenon is not only the terror of the senior golfing circuits, he is also still competing with a vengeance against the best the US pro tour has to offer. Snead doesn't play the tour as often as he once did, but he picked up $23 931 out there in the first three months of 1973, including a fourth place finish in the Jackie Gleason Inverrary Classic.

No one – including Sam – is exactly sure how many tournaments he has won around the world during his long career, but he has a record eighty-four US PGA tour events to his credit, which puts him way ahead of any other golfer in history. Since joining the tour in 1937, his victories have included three Masters and three US PGA Championships, not to mention the 1946 British Open, a handful of World Cup victories, the US Club Professionals' Championship and five US PGA Seniors' Championships. He also holds a record – which he may yet break – as the PGA's oldest tournament winner; he won the 1965 Greensboro Open when he was fifty-two years, ten months and seven days old. But perhaps the finest measure of his ability is the Vardon Trophy scoring average record he set in 1950, which is still unbeaten – 69.23.

Snead has been an omnipresent figure in American golf since 1937, but, of his contemporaries (men like Ben Hogan and Byron Nelson), he is the only one who still gets out and competes with the 'flippy-wristed' youngsters on a regular basis. Perhaps that's why he is the only golfer to have joined the tour earlier than 1952 who is in the top 25 of the US PGA's all-time money-winners' list – in nineteenth place with $624 688 at the end of 1972. To put that total in its true perspective, it should of course be mentioned that Sam frequently wins more cash today for a finish down the list than he did for victory in his heyday.

Snead has been head professional at the Greenbrier Hotel, a luxurious, tradition-steeped resort in the Virginia mountains, since 1936, and he still plays there frequently in his spare time, usually against amateurs for healthy bets. In the winter he lives in Florida, and in all seasons spends a lot of time hunting and fishing. But rarely does a day pass without Sam playing golf.

The familiar figure in the straw hat is considered by most experts to have the finest natural swing the game has ever seen – in fact, twenty-five of the top players on tour voted him the best swinger in the world in an American magazine article last year. Obviously not greatly hindered by age, he continues to make every move almost flawlessly and with matchless tempo. Occasionally troubled by arthritis in his left wrist, Snead otherwise is in superb physical shape, and is still greatly aided by his double-jointedness. Somewhat plumper than in his youth, his only golfing problem seems to be putting yips, which he has virtually cured by stroking the ball from an idiosyncratic side-saddle position.

Snead's matchless swing has always been equalled by his competitive instinct. He is always eager to go out and play, and the only way he plays – for a $5 'Nassau' or a $100 000 prize on tour – is to win. Few people in American golf doubt that he will continue to win tournaments for years to come – leaving a lot of awestruck younger players back in the dust.

Ken Bowden

1   2   3

Analysis

There are, in my view, two special reasons why Sam Snead's golf game has so remarkably stood the test of time:

1. Always possessed of a superbly athletic physique, Sam has taken great care of it, with the result that he is extremely fit and able for a man in his sixties.

2. Snead's golf swing is a totally coordinated action. In other words, there is absolutely no independent movement of one segment of his anatomy as compared to another as he swings away from and back through the ball.

In the latter respect, Snead was a trend setter when he first appeared on the tournament scene back in the 'thirties. At that time the strongest emphasis in golf technique, in America as in Britain, was on hand action. Almost everybody thought and taught 'use the hands', and although Sam certainly did (and does) use his hands, the 'one-piece' character of his overall swing represented a new style of play, from which first began to grow the modern emphasis on body action.

4   5   6

All his life Snead has tended to aim to the right at address, which promotes a big body-turn going back and, of course, produces the right-to-left flight he has generally favoured. Combined with the rearward set of his head (frames 1 and 2), Sam's setting of his shoulders 'closed' to the target line causes the club to be swung back well inside the target line (frames 2 through 4), but note how his arms swing *up into the air*, not around his body, as is the tendency of many golfers who swing the club back on the inside.

Frames 1 through 3 beautifully illustrate what is meant by a one-piece takeaway. There is no vestige here of picking the club up with the hands and wrists or lifting it with the arms. The club is worked to the top of the backswing by the winding or coiling of the upper body, with the club-hands-arms unit going along for the ride until, as the arms pass through horizontal, the weight and momentum of the clubhead begin to pull the wrists into a cocked position (frame 4).

And what a wind-up it is! The top-of-the-backswing position seen in frame 5 is, in my view, 100 per cent correct: a superb model for every physically fit weekend golfer to try to emulate. There is a degree of tilt to the shoulders here, but it is obvious that they have turned much more than they have tilted.

Snead's action is the antipathy of the exaggerated tilting shoulder action common to many of today's younger players who have been

75

7   8   9

brain-washed with the idea that the club should be swung on a straight line. Many of the moderns certainly play well for a while with those extra upright swings, but few are as *consistently* good or as *effortlessly powerful* as Sam has been, and I'd bet my bottom dollar none will last as long as he has.

Notice in frames 2 through 5 how Snead's legs resist the turning of his shoulders, until only as he reaches the top of the swing is his left heel *pulled* clear of the ground. Likewise, his hips are pulled around by his turning shoulders, rather than spun in harness with his shoulder turn – a common fault of the weekend golfer eager to make a big body turn.

Starting down, Sam's first move is to replant his left heel firmly on the ground (frame 6), which initiates the targetwards knee-shuttle (frame 7) common to all good golfers at the start of the downswing. But in studying the unwinding of the lower body, compare (especially you 'late-hit' addicts) the degree of arm-swing relative to the degree of leg and hip action. Notice particularly how much the gap between the hands and the shoulders has widened between frame 6 and frame 9, compared to the movement of Snead's hips between those two frames.

This is *release*, a much-neglected word in golf tuition, and you can see more of it in frame 9, where the uncocking of the wrists is now

76

10

11

12

delivering the clubhead on a relatively shallow arc solidly into the back of the ball. And for the ultimate depiction of what 'use the clubhead' means, compare frames 9 and 11.

We don't here see the graceful completion of this magnificent golf swing, but our final frame is a lovely illustration of the momentum of the freewheeling clubhead continuing to unwind the body, which in turn swivels the player's head so that he may watch the shot in the most natural and fluent manner.

The majority of golfers the world over, I know, look upon Sam Snead as a uniquely gifted genius who does his thing by instinct rather than through knowledge and reason. From my occasional conversations with him over the years I do not believe that to be true. To me, Sam is an extremely knowledgeable and perceptive golfer, who, when he does talk about technique, produces more good sense in fewer words than just about any player I've encountered.

John Jacobs

The authors are grateful to the following for permission to reproduce photographs of which they own the copyright:

Golf Magazine, USA
Frank Gardner
H. W. Neale
Press Association
Syndication International
Peter Dazely
Leonard Kamsler